OKLAHOMA
SOONERS

BY ALEX MONNIG

Published by ABDO Publishing Company, PO Box 398166, Minneapolis, MN 55439. Copyright © 2013 by Abdo Consulting Group, Inc. International copyrights reserved in all countries. No part of this book may be reproduced in any form without written permission from the publisher. SportsZone™ is a trademark and logo of ABDO Publishing Company.

Printed in the United States of America,
North Mankato, Minnesota
052012
092012

 THIS BOOK CONTAINS AT LEAST 10% RECYCLED MATERIALS.

Editor: Chrös McDougall
Series Designer: Craig Hinton

Photo Credits: Ty Russell/AP Images, cover, 39; AP Images, 1, 12, 20, 26, 31, 42 (bottom left), 42 (bottom right), 43 (top left), 43 (top right); J. Pat Carter/AP Images, 4, 17, 41, 42 (top); Luis M. Alvarez/ AP Images, 7; Tony Guiterrez/AP Images, 9; Amy E. Conn/AP Images, 11; Matty Zimmerman/AP Images, 18; William P. Straeter/AP Images, 22; Harold Valentine/AP Images, 25; Charles Bennett/AP Images, 29; Mark Foley/AP Images, 33; Alan Byrd/AP Images, 34; Ty Russell/The Daily Oklahoman/AP Images, 37, 43 (bottom); Sue Ogrocki/AP Images, 44

Library of Congress Cataloging-in-Publication Data
Monnig, Alex.
  Oklahoma Sooners / by Alex Monnig.
     p. cm. -- (Inside college football)
  Includes index.
  ISBN 978-1-61783-502-5
  1. University of Oklahoma--Football--History--Juvenile literature. 2. Oklahoma Sooners (Football team)--History--Juvenile literature. I. Title.
  GV958.U585M66 2013
  796.332'630976637--dc23
                    2012001854

TABLE OF CONTENTS

Oklahoma linebacker Torrance Marshall returns an interception for a touchdown during a 2000 win against Texas A&M.

STOOPS STEERS SOONERS TO SUCCESS

THE OKLAHOMA SOONERS WERE NO STRANGERS TO BEING AT THE TOP OF THE COLLEGE FOOTBALL WORLD. COMING INTO THE 2000 SEASON, THEY HAD WON SIX NATIONAL TITLES. AND THEY HAD ENJOYED SEVERAL PERIODS OF DOMINANCE SINCE THE PROGRAM STARTED IN 1895. THAT INCLUDED A RECORD 47-GAME WINNING STREAK DURING THE 1950s.

But times were tough during the 1990s in Norman, Oklahoma. The Sooners had just five winning seasons in that 10-year span. They only played in four bowl games. And they won just two.

Things were especially bad toward the end of the decade. From 1994 to 1998, the Sooners went just 23–33. So the program looked to make a coaching change ahead of the 1999 season. It went with Florida defensive coordinator Bob Stoops.

Stoops had some success during his first season. He led the team to a 7–5 record and its first bowl game in five

"RED OCTOBER"

After starting the 2000 season 4–0, the Sooners faced a difficult month against three teams ranked in the top 10 in the nation. But Oklahoma beat all three of them during what came to be known as "Red October." This included wins over second-ranked Kansas State and top-ranked Nebraska in consecutive weeks. It was the first time in National Collegiate Athletic Association (NCAA) history that a team had beaten the top two teams in the AP Poll two weeks in a row.

years. But his second year was much better. By the end of the season, the Sooners were ranked number one in the Bowl Championship Series (BCS) rankings. The BCS is a computer system used to match up the best college football teams at the end of the season.

The Orange Bowl in Miami, Florida, was considered the BCS national championship game that year. Oklahoma was set to face second-ranked Florida State there. It was a controversial selection at the time, because other polls had Miami ranked second and Florida State ranked third.

Still, the Florida State Seminoles were a formidable opponent. They had won the national championship the year before. And they had finished ranked in the top four in the Associated Press (AP) Poll 14 years in a row leading into the 2000 season. The AP Poll is one of the most respected polls for college football. So even though Oklahoma was ranked first, many people thought Florida State's fast, athletic team would win easily.

Bob Stoops
Head Coach
University of Oklahoma

Oklahoma coach Bob Stoops brought a winning tradition back to Oklahoma after he took over in 1999.

Stoops's experience coaching at Florida was a big benefit for the Sooners, though. He had helped the Florida Gators win the 1996 national championship. And he had faced the high-scoring Florida State offense several times, so he knew how to defend against it. Oklahoma fans were optimistic going into the game.

[7]

SIMILAR SQUADS

Oklahoma and Florida State had plenty of similarities heading into their 2001 Orange Bowl showdown. Florida State was 11–1. Oklahoma was 12–0. Quality quarterbacks led both teams as well. Florida State's was Chris Weinke. He won the Heisman Trophy that season. The award is given each year to the best player in college football. Senior Josh Heupel played quarterback for Oklahoma. He had finished second in the voting for the award.

Both teams were also good on both sides of the ball. Florida State was the fifth-highest-scoring team in the nation with almost 40 points per game. Oklahoma was ninth with 37 points per game. The Seminoles also had the best defense in the country. It allowed just over 10 points per game. The Sooners were fifth in the nation, allowing just less than 15 points per game.

The 76,835 fans at Pro Player Stadium that night expected the two high-flying offenses to trade scores throughout the game. Florida State's Heisman Trophy-winning quarterback Chris Weinke got the game off to a fast start. He completed a 35-yard pass to wide receiver Atrews Bell on the first play of the game. But the free-flowing nature of the game stopped there. Instead, it was the two elite defenses that took over.

Oklahoma senior linebacker Torrance Marshall intercepted a Weinke pass in the first quarter. The Sooners' offense was then able to get close enough for junior kicker Tim Duncan to hit a 27-yard field goal. That turned out to be the only scoring in the first half.

After halftime, the defenses picked up where they left off. Duncan hit another field goal in the third quarter. The 42-yard kick extended Oklahoma's lead to 6–0. And it was the only score of the quarter.

Oklahoma quarterback Josh Heupel drops back during the first quarter of the 2001 Orange Bowl against Florida State.

The Sooners finally broke through in the final 15 minutes. All-American junior linebacker Rocky Calmus caused Weinke to fumble deep in Seminoles territory. Soon after, sophomore running back Quentin Griffin busted into the end zone with 8:30 to play. That put Oklahoma up 13–0.

Florida State was able to register a safety with 55 seconds left in the game. That cut the score to 13–2. But it was too little, too late. That score held as Sooners senior defensive back Ontei Jones intercepted Weinke with 16 seconds left to end the contest.

"Our players recognize that the history of Oklahoma is winning championships," Stoops said after the game. "We already had six, now we have seven."

Oklahoma senior quarterback Josh Heupel did not have great numbers. But he had done enough to give the Oklahoma defense a rest. He completed 25 of 39 passes for 214 yards. More importantly, he kept the ball away from the high-powered Florida State offense. The Sooners had the ball on offense for 13 more minutes than Florida State.

Like they had done all year, the Sooners won the game with their suffocating defense. Marshall made six tackles to go along with his interception. He was named the game's Most Valuable Player (MVP). Oklahoma disguised its coverages all night. The Sooners had players pretend they were going to rush the quarterback, then drop back to

STOOPS'S BOWL STREAK

Bob Stoops had tremendous success as a defensive coordinator at Florida. He brought that success with him to Oklahoma when he became coach before the 1999 season. In his first 13 years, he brought the Sooners to bowl games every season. That included eight appearances in BCS games.

cover receivers. "It seemed like they had radar," Bell said after the game. "Everything we tried they were ready for."

The win left Oklahoma as the only undefeated team in the country. It also left it as national champion for the seventh time. In just his second year, Stoops had brought the Sooners back to the top of the college football world. And he was only the most recent in a long line of successful coaches at Oklahoma.

STOOPS STEERS SOONERS TO SUCCESS

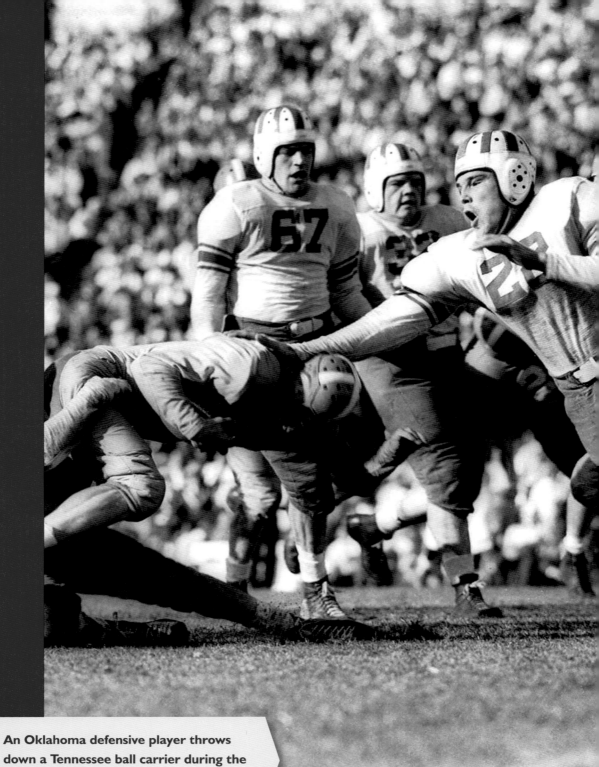

An Oklahoma defensive player throws down a Tennessee ball carrier during the Orange Bowl on January 2, 1939.

A SMALL START

OKLAHOMA PLAYED ITS FIRST-EVER FOOTBALL GAME ON NOVEMBER 7, 1895. THE OPPONENT WAS A TEAM FROM NEARBY OKLAHOMA CITY. IT WAS MADE UP OF LOCAL HIGH SCHOOL PLAYERS AND PLAYERS FROM NEARBY METHODIST COLLEGE. BUT THE OKLAHOMA CITY TEAM BEAT UP ON OKLAHOMA IN A 34–0 WIN.

College football, both as a sport and in its organization, was very different in its early years. The game itself resembled rugby more than today's football. There were also no massive stadiums, prime time television coverage, or major conferences. For the next four years, the team played at least two games per season. The opponents were teams from nearby places such as Arkansas, Texas, and Oklahoma. The team, then sometimes known as the Rough Riders, went 8–2 in those first five years.

Vernon L. Parrington became Oklahoma's first full-time football coach in 1897. Parrington made sure the team lived

RABID RIVALRIES

The Sooners have piled up hundreds of victories over the years. And they have managed to make a few enemies along the way. One of Oklahoma's biggest rivals is Texas. It is known as the Red River Rivalry.

Since their first meeting in 1900, the teams have become two of the most successful programs in the history of college football. In 1912, the game in which they play each other was moved to Dallas, Texas, because of its size and importance.

The Sooners also have a strong rivalry with Oklahoma State. Those two meet every year in what is known as the Bedlam Series. The first Bedlam game was in 1904. Oklahoma beat Oklahoma State—which was then known as Oklahoma A&M—75–0. It remained the biggest win in the history of the series through 2011. The series has been lopsided through 2011, with Oklahoma holding an all-time record of 82–17–7.

up to its Rough Riders name. He ran hard practices and made the players spend a lot of time on the field.

Oklahoma started playing more games in 1900. Perhaps the most important one was on October 10 of that year. That is when Oklahoma played Texas for the first time. Texas won the game 28–2. But the teams would go on to play each other many more times over the next 100-plus years. Many consider their annual Red River Rivalry to be one of the best in college football. The Red River runs along part of the Oklahoma-Texas border.

A major turning point in school history took place in 1905, when Bennie Owen took over as coach. He coached the team from 1905 to 1926. Through 2011, no coach has led the Sooners for longer. During those 21 seasons, the team went 122–54–16. Another important Oklahoma tradition began in 1908. That is when the school's sports teams adopted the "Sooners" nickname.

The Sooners won a lot of games under Owen. And the players leading the team started to get some national recognition. In 1913, senior fullback Claude Reeds became the first Sooner to be named an All-American. Reeds was technically a fullback. However, he confused teams by often throwing the ball. He sometimes played end as well, and he even punted for the Sooners.

Two of Owen's best seasons came when Oklahoma joined the Southwest Conference in 1914. The team went 9–1–1 in its first year in the conference. Then in 1915, the Sooners went 10–0. They tied with Baylor for their first conference championship. Three years later, they again tied for the conference championship, this time with Texas.

The Sooners spent six years in the Southwest Conference. Then, in 1920, they joined the Missouri Valley Intercollegiate Athletic Association (MVIAA). They got started on the right foot with a 6–0–1 season. That was good enough to win the conference title. Two All-Americans, halfback Phil White and tackle Roy "Soupy" Smoot, led the way.

WHAT IS A SOONER?

The term Sooner was created around the time of the Civil War. Back in the 1860s, the United States was issuing new land for people to settle on. There was a specific day and time that people were allowed to go claim it. Sooners were people who tried to go claim the land too early. The term came to mean somebody who was energetic and a hard worker. In 1908, Oklahoma's sports teams officially adopted the Sooners nickname. The name was taken from a pep club called the Sooner Rooters.

The Sooners spent eight years in the MVIAA. Then they became one of the first members of the new Big Six Conference. Although the league would change names as it added teams over the years, it remained the Sooners' conference through 2011.

Owen retired as Oklahoma's football coach after the 1926 season, just before the Big Six move. He decided to instead become the school's athletic director. But his influence was felt during every single home game for years to come. That is because Owen helped organize the funding to pay for what became the school's football field complex. In 1923, the field was named Owen Field in honor of the coach.

Even though he was still around the university, Owen's presence on the sidelines was missed. The Sooners had just 11 winning seasons over the next 20 years. Owen only had four non-winning seasons during his 26 years in charge. Coaches Adrian Lindsey, Lewie Hardage, and Biff Jones did not have much luck leading the Sooners. But Tom Stidham briefly turned around the program when he coached from 1937 to 1940.

OWEN FIELD

The Sooners started playing at the site of Oklahoma Memorial Stadium before it was even finished. The team played its first game at that location in 1923. It was then that the school named the field Owen Field. Two years later, it played in front of the stands for the first time. Initially, the stadium only had 16,000 seats. Now 82,112 people can fit inside to watch the Sooners play. Memorial Stadium is named in honor of people from the school who had died in World War I.

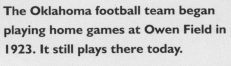

The Oklahoma football team began playing home games at Owen Field in 1923. It still plays there today.

It was under Stidham that Oklahoma went to its first bowl game: the Orange Bowl after the 1938 season. There, Tennessee shut out the Sooners 17–0. That was Oklahoma's only loss of the year. Still, the team finished 10–1 and ranked fourth in the final AP Poll. The next year, Oklahoma finished 6–2–1, earning it a nineteenth ranking in the AP Poll. It was the last time the Sooners would be ranked for a while.

The Sooners went through five up-and-down years under coach Snorter Luster. Then Jim Tatum stepped in and took the Sooners to their second bowl game in 1946. Oklahoma beat North Carolina State 34–13 in the Gator Bowl. It was the Sooners' first bowl victory, and it finished off an 8–3 season. But once again, it was time for a new coach to take over. In came Bud Wilkinson, and everything changed.

The American Football Coaches Association named Oklahoma coach Bud Wilkinson the 1949 Coach of the Year.

WILKINSON'S WINNING STREAK

OKLAHOMA HAD NOT BEEN ABLE TO WIN CONSISTENTLY SINCE BENNIE OWEN'S MOVE TO ATHLETIC DIRECTOR. THE TEAM WENT THROUGH SIX COACHES IN THE 21 YEARS FOLLOWING OWEN'S SWITCH. NONE OF THEM HAD STAYED ON LONGER THAN FIVE YEARS.

Oklahoma finally found a lasting coach in Bud Wilkinson. Wilkinson joined the Oklahoma staff in 1946 as an assistant coach under his friend Jim Tatum. He became head coach when Tatum left one year later. Over the course of his career, Wilkinson would lead the Sooners to places that no other team in college football had gone before.

"If you have the will to prepare, things will usually work out quite well, and the will to win will take care of itself," Wilkinson said.

It quickly became clear that the Sooners had the will. In just his second year, Wilkinson led Oklahoma to a

10–1 season. That included a 14–6 win over North Carolina in the Sugar Bowl following the 1948 season. Oklahoma went back to the Sugar Bowl after the 1949 and 1950 seasons as well. But it was the last one that was most important.

In 1949, the Sooners had finished the season undefeated. Wilkinson was named Coach of the Year. The only problem was that Notre Dame had been undefeated, too. As such, the Sooners ended up finishing second in the final AP Poll. There was no dedicated national championship game at the time, so Notre Dame claimed the title.

There would be no finishing second the next year for Oklahoma, though. The Sooners made it through the 1950 regular season undefeated. That included wins over three ranked teams. Oklahoma had four All-Americans on its roster that year. Fullback Leon Heath and tackle Jim Weatherall led the eighth-highest-scoring offense in the country. Safety Buddy Jones and end Frankie Anderson anchored the defense.

Oklahoma earned a chance to try to win its third Sugar Bowl in a row. But the offense fell flat in a 13–7 loss to third-ranked Kentucky. College football can often be unpredictable, though. In the season's final AP Poll, the 10–1 Sooners were still named the national champions. And Wilkinson was just getting started.

The 1953 Sooners started the season with a loss and a tie. But a 19–14 win over Texas got the ball rolling. That momentum would not stop for a while. From 1953 to 1957, the Sooners won 47 straight games. No other team has ever matched that feat through 2011. Many consider that five-year stretch to be the most successful in college football history.

BILLY VESSELS

In 1952, senior halfback Billy "Curly" Vessels became the first Oklahoma player to win the Heisman Trophy. He ran for 1,072 yards and 17 touchdowns, caught seven passes for 165 yards and a touchdown, and even completed seven passes for two touchdowns that season. Vessels is one of the big reasons why the Sooners led the nation in scoring that year, with just over 40 points per game.

WILKINSON'S WINNING STREAK

Oklahoma's Tommy McDonald runs around the Kansas defense during a 1954 game in Kansas. The Sooners won 65–0.

The Sooners finished the 1953 season 9–1–1. They ranked in the top 10 in the country in scoring and allowed the fourth fewest points per game. Oklahoma maintained its spot in the top 10 in both areas for the next three years. In 1954, Oklahoma went a perfect 10–0. But several other teams were also undefeated that season, and Oklahoma finished third in the AP Poll.

A lot of key players from the 1954 undefeated team had been seniors. Wilkinson did not expect the winning streak to continue. "I don't think we're going to be nearly as good a football team as people think," he said before the start of the 1955 season. But he was wrong. The Sooners scored 35 points per game that season. That was more than any other team in the country. And they had the defense to match. Oklahoma allowed less than six points per game.

On January 2, 1956, Wilkinson led the top-ranked Sooners against third-ranked Maryland in the Orange Bowl. Both teams were undefeated. But some people did not think Oklahoma was as good as its record showed. That is because the 1955 Sooners had only played two ranked teams. But the team proved its top ranking by beating Maryland 20–6 that night in Miami. Wilkinson had led the team to a second national championship.

"That's the most satisfying victory we've ever had," Wilkinson said after the game. "Everyone has been talking about how weak a schedule we play, and they're justified in doing so. We didn't know if we were good enough to play a team like Maryland or not. Now we know . . ."

The win streak was at 30 when Oklahoma opened the 1956 season. All-American senior halfback/defensive back Tommy McDonald once

RAMPANT RUSHING

All-American halfback Tommy McDonald led the Sooners in rushing for the second straight season in 1956, when he ran for 853 yards. But he could not have done it without the help of All-American guards Ed Gray and Bill Krisher and All-American center Jerry Tubbs. "Our line is the best," McDonald said. "I'm proud to run behind them."

WILKINSON'S WINNING STREAK

SOONERS

BUD WILKINSON

Bud Wilkinson spent 17 years coaching at Oklahoma. He led the team to a 145–29–4 record, including a 6–2 record in bowl games. The Sooners won an incredible 47 games in a row from 1953 to 1957. But that was not Wilkinson's only streak. The Sooners were also undefeated in 74 conference games from 1946 to 1959 (Jim Tatum was still coach in 1946). They went 72–0–2 during that span and won 14 straight conference championships starting in 1946.

Wilkinson built teams made from players found in the middle of the country. He only recruited within approximately 150 miles (241 km) of Oklahoma's campus in Norman. Even with those self-imposed limits, he was able to win the school its first three championships in 1950, 1955, and 1956.

again led the Sooners' offense. He had become the first Oklahoma player to score a touchdown in every game of a season in 1955. He also led the team in rushing yards and was named an All-American that year. In 1956, he again accomplished both things.

The Sooners' rushing attack helped them score more than 46 points per game. That led the nation for the second year in a row. And just like in 1955, the defense only gave up about five points per game and ranked second in the country. It shut out six teams that season, helping the team win every game except two by at least 36 points. Oklahoma came into the season ranked first in the AP Poll. And its 10–0 record made sure it ended the season that way. The Sooners were champions for a third time.

For a lot of 1957, it looked like Oklahoma was going to complete another undefeated season. The Sooners won their first seven games to

push the winning streak to 47. But it finally came to an end. Notre Dame came to town and beat Oklahoma 7–0.

Still, the Sooners went on to go 10–1, win the Orange Bowl, and finish fourth in the nation. Oklahoma had a similar season in 1958. It once again finished 10–1 and won the Orange Bowl.

But even Wilkinson went through some tough times. The Sooners went a combined 31–19 over the next five years. Many teams would be happy with that record. However, it was a step down for the Sooners, and it included two losing seasons. Wilkinson finally retired from coaching after the 1963 season. But it was not long before a new coach came and took the Sooners back to the top.

Oklahoma running back Steve Owens bulldozes through two Tennessee defenders during the 1968 Orange Bowl.

4

SWITZER'S SOONERS

BUD WILKINSON HAD TURNED OKLAHOMA INTO ONE OF THE BEST COLLEGE FOOTBALL PROGRAMS IN THE COUNTRY. BUT THE SOONERS HAD TROUBLE KEEPING THE TRADITION GOING IN THE YEARS IMMEDIATELY AFTER WILKINSON LEFT. AFTER THREE DISAPPOINTING SEASONS, CHUCK FAIRBANKS WAS NAMED HEAD COACH IN 1967. AND HE QUICKLY TURNED AROUND THE TEAM.

One of the reasons for the turnaround was running back Steve Owens. He played for Oklahoma from 1967 to 1969. His last season was his best. In it, he ran for 1,523 yards and scored 23 touchdowns. It was enough to earn him the Heisman Trophy.

Fairbanks began to use a style of offense called the wishbone in 1970. It was a rushing attack that other teams had a lot of trouble stopping. Fairbanks's best seasons with Oklahoma were 1971 and 1972. The Sooners' offense in 1971 was one of the best college football had ever seen. The team averaged 566.5 yards per game and broke several records that season. Oklahoma's only loss came against Nebraska in "The Game of the Century."

The teams were becoming fierce rivals after playing many important games against each other in recent years. Both came into the 1971 Thanksgiving Day game undefeated. Nebraska was ranked first and Oklahoma was ranked second. The winner would go to the Orange Bowl. Nebraska scored in the final minutes of the game to steal a 35–31 victory from the Sooners. Oklahoma went on to win the Sugar Bowl, finish 11–1, and end the season ranked second in the final AP Poll behind Nebraska.

The 1972 Sooners had another great season. They again finished 11–1. Their only stumble came against ninth-ranked Colorado in the Sooners' fifth game of the season. But Oklahoma beat six other ranked teams that year, including fifth-ranked Penn State in the Sugar Bowl. As such, the Sooners again found themselves ranked second at the end of the season.

CHUCK FAIRBANKS

Bud Wilkinson and Barry Switzer might have had more long-term success at Oklahoma, but Chuck Fairbanks accomplished a lot in his six years as coach. He led the Sooners to a 52–15–1 record. That included a 34–8 conference record and a 3–1–1 mark in bowl games. Through 2011, his .772 career winning percentage remained the fourth highest in Sooners history among coaches who led the team for at least five seasons.

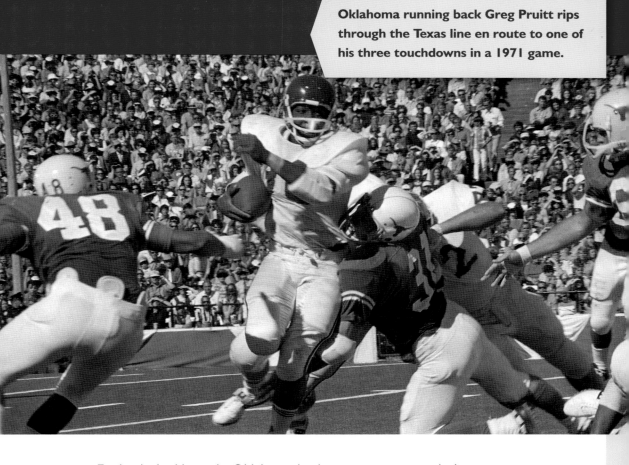

Oklahoma running back Greg Pruitt rips through the Texas line en route to one of his three touchdowns in a 1971 game.

Fairbanks had brought Oklahoma back to prominence with the wishbone offense. He was so successful that people outside college football were taking notice. In 1973, he left Oklahoma for the New England Patriots in the National Football League (NFL). But the Sooners did not miss a beat with new coach Barry Switzer.

Switzer had been Oklahoma's offensive coordinator since 1967. He was one of the masterminds behind the Sooners' use of the wishbone formation. And he continued to run the offense well as head coach. In fact, Switzer's first year was almost perfect. Running backs Waymon Clark and Joe Washington carried on the rushing tradition by running for

THE WISHBONE OFFENSE

In 1968, Texas assistant Emory Bellard created the wishbone formation to take advantage of the Longhorns' talented running backs. The wishbone formation uses three running backs. They line up in a "Y" shape—the same general shape as a wishbone in a turkey. The fullback lines up behind the quarterback. The other two backs line up behind the fullback on either side. This gives the quarterback three different players to which he can hand off the ball. In 1970, Sooners coach Chuck Fairbanks and offensive coordinator Barry Switzer decided to use the formation at Oklahoma.

more than 1,000 yards each. Sophomore quarterback Steve Davis was also dangerous with his legs. He tallied up 887 yards on the ground. The Sooners finished the 1973 season 10–0–1 and third in the AP Poll.

Nobody stopped the Sooners in 1974. They led the nation in offense with 43 points per game. They also finished fifth in the nation in scoring defense, allowing just over eight points per game. Oklahoma was ranked first in the preseason AP Poll. It ended the season that way, too. Oklahoma went a perfect 11–0 and won its fourth national title.

Switzer and the Sooners were not done winning championships. The team won its first eight games in the next season. That gave Switzer a 30-game unbeaten streak to start his head-coaching career. But the streak came to an end in his thirty-first game in charge. Kansas upset Oklahoma at home 23–3.

The Sooners won their next two games and earned a spot in the Orange Bowl. They were ranked third and met fifth-ranked Michigan.

Oklahoma halfback Billy Sims rushes past Kansas defenders during a 1979 game. He won the 1978 Heisman Trophy.

It was a tight, low-scoring contest. Oklahoma came away with a 14–6 win. Luckily for the Sooners, the University of California, Los Angeles Bruins beat top-ranked Ohio State in the Rose Bowl. That led to Oklahoma once again being voted as the top team in the nation. The Sooners had not been perfect. But they had been good enough to become the first team in NCAA history to win back-to-back championships twice.

The wins kept coming for Switzer and the Sooners over the next five years. The team did not drop more than two games in any of those seasons. And it finished in the top 10 of the AP Poll each year. The Sooners were 4–1 in bowl games during that span, winning the Fiesta Bowl once and the Orange Bowl three times. In 1978, junior halfback Billy Sims had one of the best seasons in Oklahoma history. He scored

SWITZER'S SOONERS

THE SELMON BROTHERS

Brothers Lucious, Dewey, and Lee Roy Selmon helped Barry Switzer get off to an undefeated start as head coach at Oklahoma. Lucious was the oldest of the three. He was an All-American nose guard in 1973. He also won the Chevrolet Defensive Player of the Year Award that year. The New England Patriots—led by former Sooners coach Chuck Fairbanks—selected him in the 1974 NFL Draft. The family's influence at Oklahoma carried on with nose guard Dewey and defensive tackle Lee Roy. Both were key to the Sooners' back-to-back championships in 1974 and 1975. Both were also All-Americans during those championship years. The two kept playing together after college was over. The Tampa Bay Buccaneers took Lee Roy first overall in the 1976 NFL Draft. They then took Dewey, who was one year older, in the second round.

20 touchdowns and set a Big Eight Conference rushing record with 1,762 yards. Sims won the Heisman Trophy that season. He was also named an All-American for the first of two times.

After a brief rough patch, the Sooners got back to their best in 1985. As usual, strong rushing led the offense. Freshman quarterback Jamelle Holieway guided the wishbone attack. He threw for 517 yards and rushed for 862. Sophomore running back Lydell Carr led the team in rushing with 883 yards. And players such as All-Americans sophomore linebacker Brian Bosworth, senior defensive end Kevin Murphy, and senior tackle Tony Casillas led the defense. It ranked second in the nation.

The Sooners had come into the season ranked first in the AP Poll. But they lost to the Miami Hurricanes in the fourth week of the season. That would be Oklahoma's only loss that year. The Sooners fought their way back up to a number-three ranking.

Oklahoma players carry coach Barry Switzer off the field following the Sooners' 1986 Orange Bowl win.

That earned them the right to play top-ranked Penn State in the Orange Bowl. Bosworth and the rest of the defense held Penn State to just one touchdown in a 25–10 win. The Sooners had done enough to regain the number-one ranking in the final AP Poll. They were champions for the sixth time in school history.

Oklahoma had talented teams in 1986 and 1987. Each year they came into the season ranked first in the AP Poll. Just like in 1985, they lost one game each season. Both times it was again to Miami. The Hurricanes handed the Sooners their only loss of the season three seasons in a row. Switzer stuck around for one more year. But the next 10 seasons would be among the hardest in team history.

Oklahoma's Corey Mayfield dances across the field following the team's win over Virginia in the 1991 Gator Bowl.

5

ONWARD, OKLAHOMA

BARRY SWITZER WAS THE FOURTH-WINNINGEST COACH IN
NCAA FOOTBALL HISTORY WHEN HE LEFT OKLAHOMA. HE
HAD BROUGHT THE SOONERS AND THEIR FANS GREAT SUCCESS
DURING HIS YEARS WITH THE PROGRAM. BUT IT WAS NOT IN
GREAT SHAPE WHEN HE LEFT. THE NCAA PUT OKLAHOMA ON
PROBATION FOR THREE YEARS FOR BREAKING RECRUITING RULES.
THE SOONERS WERE NOT ALLOWED TO PLAY ON TELEVISION
IN 1989. THEY COULD NOT PLAY IN BOWL GAMES IN 1989 OR
1990. AND THERE WERE OTHER LIMITS PUT ON HOW MUCH TIME
COACHES COULD SPEND WITH RECRUITS.

The punishments kept Oklahoma from getting the
top-flight athletes to which the program was accustomed.
That lack of new recruits showed on the field. From 1989
to 1998, the team finished its seasons ranked in the AP Poll
only three times. The Sooners were seventeenth in 1990,
sixteenth in 1991, and seventeenth again in 1993. Oklahoma
fans had gotten used to seeing stars on the field. After all,
there had been seasons where eight Sooners had been

BOB STOOPS

It did not take Bob Stoops long to show that he belonged in the same category as other great Oklahoma coaches, such as Bud Wilkinson and Barry Switzer. He led the Sooners to their seventh national championship in just his second year in charge. But what is maybe more impressive is how he has been able to keep the wins coming. In his first 13 seasons, through 2011, Stoops compiled a 139–34 record. His teams reached the national championship game four times. He also had a good record against Oklahoma's two biggest rivals. Through 2011, Stoops's Sooners were 18–8 against Texas and Oklahoma State. Perhaps Stoops's only shortcoming as a coach is his bowl record. Oklahoma has played in a bowl game every year since his arrival. But the team was just 7–6 in those games.

named All-Americans. But during that 10-season stretch, Oklahoma had only two.

The program hit a low point in 1994. That year started a string of five straight non-winning seasons. Never before had the program gone through such a stretch. But then Bob Stoops arrived in 1999 from Florida. In just his second year, he helped lead the Sooners to their seventh national championship.

One of the main reasons behind the quick turnaround was the team's commitment to defense. From 2000 to 2003, the Sooners were among the nation's top six teams in points allowed. Stoops had worked as a defensive coordinator for 10 years at Kansas State and Florida before coming to Oklahoma. He coached some of the best defensive players in Oklahoma's history during those years. Linebackers Rocky Calmus and Teddy Lehman and defensive tackle Tommie Harris were each All-Americans twice during that four-season stretch.

That defense helped keep the Sooners near the top of the AP Poll in the four seasons after the 2000 national championship. But each year, the team came up just short of winning it all. In 2003, the Sooners had a powerful offense to match their tough defense. Junior quarterback Jason White broke the school record for touchdown passes in a season with 40. He also became Oklahoma's fourth Heisman Trophy winner.

The Sooners won their first 12 games of the season. But they stumbled in the Big 12 Championship Game. Kansas State blew them out 35–7. Many fans were upset when the BCS still ranked Oklahoma

ROCKY CALMUS

Linebacker Rocky Calmus led the Sooners in tackles during his sophomore, junior, and senior years. He was an All-American as a junior in 2000 and as a senior in 2001. He also won the Dick Butkus Award in 2001. It is given each year to the best linebacker in the country. But perhaps the most impressive thing about Calmus was his toughness. He played most of the 2000 season with a broken bone near his thumb.

as the number-one team. After all, the Sooners had not even won their conference. But either way, the team traveled to New Orleans, Louisiana, to face Louisiana State in the Sugar Bowl. The game was also the BCS national championship. However, Oklahoma again stumbled. It was only able to gain 154 yards on offense in a 21–14 loss.

White had another outstanding year in 2004. He threw for 3,205 yards and 35 touchdowns. Joining him in the backfield was standout freshman running back Adrian Peterson. The All-American ran for 1,925 yards and 15 touchdowns. It was one of the best freshman college football seasons ever. Peterson finished second in Heisman Trophy voting, while White finished third.

White and Peterson led the Sooners to another undefeated regular season in 2004. This time they won the Big 12 championship, crushing Colorado 42–3 in the conference title game. So Oklahoma advanced to the Orange Bowl to face the University of Southern California (USC). The Orange Bowl served as the BCS title game that year. But the game was not close. Oklahoma could not stop USC's junior quarterback Matt

Leinart, who had won the Heisman Trophy that year. Leinart threw for five touchdowns to crush Oklahoma's title dreams in a 55–19 loss.

Stoops had taken Oklahoma to the national championship game three times in his first six seasons as coach. And it would not be long before he had the Sooners back there. In 2007, three years after White graduated, another talented quarterback took over the team. Freshman Sam Bradford led an offense that scored more than 42 points per game. He threw for 3,121 yards and 36 touchdowns. That was just four fewer than White had thrown for during his school-record-setting 2003 Heisman season.

Bradford destroyed White's numbers the next season. In fact, Bradford had what might have been the best season by a quarterback in Sooners' history. In 2008, he threw for 4,720 yards and 50 touchdowns. He also won that year's Heisman Trophy. Along with Bradford, All-American junior tight end Jermaine Gresham and running backs sophomore Demarco Murray and junior Chris Brown helped the Sooners score just more than 51 points per game. That was the most in the country. The Sooners made the national championship game for the fourth time in Stoops's career as coach. But once again, the Sooners could not make the final push to get back to the top. Oklahoma lost 24–14 to Florida.

Bradford left for the NFL Draft after the 2009 season. Still, the Sooners remained one of the top teams in the country. Behind sophomore quarterback Landry Jones, Oklahoma won 12 games in 2010. That included a 48–20 win over Connecticut in the Fiesta Bowl. After

RECORD-SMASHING SAM

In just two seasons, Sam Bradford accomplished what it took previous Heisman Trophy-winner Jason White a whole college career to do. Bradford's 50 touchdowns in 2008 were 10 more than White's single-season record from just five years earlier. And Bradford's 86 touchdown passes over his first two seasons broke White's Oklahoma career touchdown record of 81. Bradford returned for his junior year, but he was injured early in the season. He finished his Oklahoma career with 88 touchdown passes. The St. Louis Rams selected him first in the 2010 NFL Draft.

starting the 2011 season ranked number one, the Sooners stumbled a bit down the stretch. Still, they won 10 games. It was their tenth time with double-digit wins since 2000.

Although the Sooners had not yet been back to a national championship game since 2008, they continued to be among the best teams in the nation. With Stoops's ability to attract top talent to a program with a long and storied history, it will likely not be long before the Sooners find themselves in another championship game.

ONWARD, OKLAHOMA

TIMELINE

On November 7, Oklahoma plays its first game in school history. It is a 34–0 loss to a team from Oklahoma City.

On October 10, Oklahoma loses 28–2 to Texas in the first game of the Red River Rivalry.

On November 6, Oklahoma beats Oklahoma State (then known as Oklahoma A&M) 75–0 in the first game of the Bedlam Series.

Fullback Claude Reeds becomes the first Sooners player to earn All-America honors.

The Sooners play their first game on Owen Field at the site of what is now known as Oklahoma Memorial Stadium.

1895   1900   1904   1913   1923

Senior running back Steve Owens wins the second Heisman Trophy in school history.

Impressed by the success of rival Texas, Oklahoma offensive coordinator Barry Switzer helps convince coach Chuck Fairbanks to start using the wishbone offense.

On September 15, Switzer coaches his first game as head coach of the Sooners. It is a 42–14 victory over Baylor.

On November 30, Oklahoma beats rival Oklahoma State 44–13 to complete another undefeated season and finish first in the AP Poll for the team's fourth national championship.

Junior halfback Billy Sims wins Oklahoma's third Heisman Trophy, leads the nation in rushing, and sets a Big Eight single-season rushing record with 1,762 yards.

1969   1970   1973   1974   1978

Oklahoma plays in its first bowl game, a 17–0 loss to Tennessee in the Orange Bowl on January 2.

Bud Wilkinson takes over as the Sooners' coach.

Billy "Curly" Vessels wins Oklahoma's first Heisman Trophy.

On October 10, the Sooners defeat rival Texas 19–14 to start Oklahoma's 47-game winning streak.

On November 16, Notre Dame beats Oklahoma 7–0 in Norman to end the Sooners' 47-game winning streak.

1939 1947 1952 1953 1957

On January 1, the Sooners beat Penn State to finish the season 11–1 and win their sixth national championship.

In just his second season, Bob Stoops guides the Sooners to a national championship in January 2001.

Senior quarterback Jason White leads the nation's top offense and wins the Heisman Trophy.

Sophomore quarterback Sam Bradford throws for 4,720 yards and 50 touchdowns and becomes the fifth Sooners player to win the Heisman Trophy.

Wide receiver Ryan Broyles is named an All-American for the second year in a row.

1986 2000 2003 2008 2011

QUICK STATS

PROGRAM INFO

University of Oklahoma Rough Riders, Boomers (1898–1908)
University of Oklahoma Sooners (1908–)

NATIONAL CHAMPIONSHIPS
(* DENOTES SHARED TITLE)

1950, 1955, 1956, 1974*, 1975, 1985, 2000

OTHER ACHIEVEMENTS

BCS bowl appearances (1999–): 8
Big 12 championships (1996–): 7
Bowl record: 27–17–1

HEISMAN TROPHY WINNERS

Billy Vessels, 1952
Steve Owens, 1969
Billy Sims, 1978
Jason White, 2003
Sam Bradford, 2008

KEY PLAYERS
(POSITION[S]; SEASONS WITH TEAM)

Brian Bosworth (LB; 1983–86)
Sam Bradford (QB; 2007–09)
Rocky Calmus (LB; 1998–2001)

* All statistics through 2011 season

Josh Heupel (QB; 1999–2000)
Keith Jackson (TE; 1984–87)
Tommy McDonald (HB; 1954–56)
Steve Owens (RB; 1967–69)
Adrian Peterson (RB; 2004–06)
Lee Roy Selmon (DT; 1972–75)
Billy Sims (HB; 1975–79)
Billy Vessels (HB; 1950–52)
Jason White (QB; 1999–2004)

KEY COACHES

Bob Stoops (1999–):
    139–34; 7–6 (bowl games)
Barry Switzer (1973–88):
    157–29–4; 8–5 (bowl games)
Bud Wilkinson (1947–63):
    145–29–4; 6–2 (bowl games)

HOME STADIUM

Oklahoma Memorial Stadium (1923–)

Bud Wilkinson stayed busy after he left the sidelines at Oklahoma. He retired from coaching to run for the US Senate, but that was unsuccessful. So he became a sports analyst on ABC television from 1965 to 1977. During that time, Wilkinson, who had a master's degree in English, was a member of the White House staff from 1969 to 1971. But he just could not keep himself away from football. He returned to coaching for two years, in 1978 and 1979, when he coached the St. Louis Cardinals in the NFL.

Brian Bosworth was one of the best linebackers to ever play college football. He was also one of the most controversial. He was known for his crazy hairstyles and for sharing his opinions about everything no matter who might be offended. Before the 1987 Orange Bowl, Bosworth was suspended for using steroids. Then on the day of the game, he wore a shirt that compared the NCAA to communists. Oklahoma coach Barry Switzer decided to kick him off the team.

"Whatever is said before, during, or after has no effect on the game. It's what happens during the 60 minutes of the game, out there on the floor of the Cotton Bowl that counts. This is no ordinary game, as anyone who has ever played or seen it would tell you." —Oklahoma Sooners coach Barry Switzer on the Red River Rivalry with Texas. The Oklahoma-Texas game was held in the Cotton Bowl stadium for many years.

GLOSSARY

All-American
A player chosen as one of the best amateurs in the country in a particular activity.

athletic director
An administrator who oversees the coaches, players, and teams of an institution.

conference
In sports, a group of teams that plays each other each season.

draft
A system used by professional sports leagues to select new players in order to spread incoming talent among all teams. The NFL Draft is held each spring.

momentum
A continued strong performance based on recent success.

probation
A period of time where a person or team tries to make up for wrongdoing.

recruit
To entice a player to come to a certain school to play on its football team. A player being sought after is known as a recruit.

recruiting
Trying to entice a player to come to a certain school.

retire
To officially end one's career.

rivalry
When opposing teams bring out great emotion in each team, its fans, and its players.

rivals
Opponents that bring out great emotion in a team, its fans, and its players.

upset
A result where the supposedly worse team defeats the supposedly better team.

FOR MORE INFORMATION

FURTHER READING

Dozier, Ray. *The Oklahoma Football Encyclopedia*. Champaign, IL: Sports Pub., 2006.

Fletcher, Jim. *The Die-Hard Fan's Guide to Sooner Football*. Washington DC: Regnery Pub., 2008.

Schroeder, George. *Game Day: Oklahoma Football*. Chicago: Triumph Books, 2006.

WEB LINKS

To learn more about the Oklahoma Sooners, visit ABDO Publishing Company online at **www.abdopublishing.com**. Web sites about the Sooners are featured on our Book Links page. These links are routinely monitored and updated to provide the most current information available.

PLACES TO VISIT

College Football Hall of Fame
111 South St. Joseph St.
South Bend, IN 46601
1-800-440-FAME (3263)
www.collegefootball.org

This hall of fame and museum highlights the greatest players and moments in the history of college football. Among the former Sooners enshrined here are Billy Vessels, Steve Owens, Keith Jackson, Lee Roy Selmon, and Joe Washington.

Oklahoma Memorial Stadium
180 W. Brooks
Norman, OK 73019
405-325-2424
www.soonersports.com/facilities/memorial-stadium.html

This has been Oklahoma's home field since 1923. It was named in honor of Oklahomans who died in World War I. After several major renovations, the stadium holds 82,112 spectators. Tours are available seven days a week.

INDEX

ABOUT THE AUTHOR

Alex Monnig is a freelance journalist from St. Louis, Missouri. He graduated with his master's degree from the University of Missouri in May 2010. He has covered sporting events around the world, including the 2008 Olympic Games in China, the 2010 Commonwealth Games in India, and the 2011 Rugby World Cup in New Zealand.